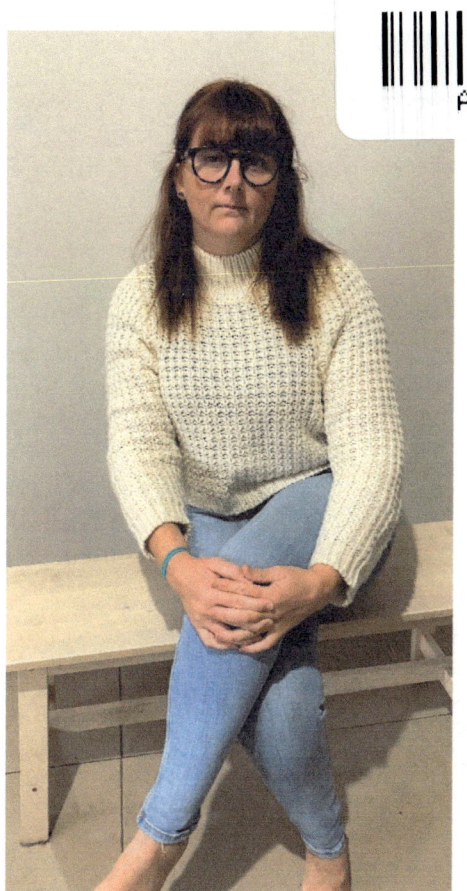

About the Author

I am a swimmer, a nurse, a mother, a lover, and a friend. I was also diagnosed with bipolar at thirty-eight years of age, so I've squeezed a lot into this short manic life. I am English-born living in Melbourne, Australia. I love the Melbourne culture and feel that that has been an inspiration to my writing. You don't have to look very far for inspiration in Melbourne.

The Human Experience

Kelly Higgins

The Human Experience

Olympia Publishers
London

www.olympiapublishers.com
OLYMPIA PAPERBACK EDITION

Copyright © Kelly Higgins 2023

The right of Kelly Higgins to be identified as author of
this work has been asserted in accordance with sections 77 and 78 of
the Copyright, Designs and Patents Act 1988.

All Rights Reserved

No reproduction, copy or transmission of this publication
may be made without written permission.
No paragraph of this publication may be reproduced,
copied or transmitted save with the written permission of the publisher,
or in accordance with the provisions
of the Copyright Act 1956 (as amended).

Any person who commits any unauthorised act in relation to
this publication may be liable to criminal
prosecution and civil claims for damage.

A CIP catalogue record for this title is
available from the British Library.

ISBN: 978-1-80439-193-8

This is a work of fiction.
Names, characters, places and incidents originate from the writer's
imagination. Any resemblance to actual persons, living or dead, is
purely coincidental.

First Published in 2023

Olympia Publishers
Tallis House
2 Tallis Street
London
EC4Y 0AB

Printed in Great Britain

Dedication

I dedicate this book to my mum and dad, sister, Lauren, my girls, my good friend, Naomi, and my electric blanket.

This book is about navigating life in a human flesh suit. Warning: this is not a guide. It involves asking a lot of questions, most of which remain unanswered, and therefore resulting in even more questions (if that isn't philosophy, I don't know what is). This book explores a deep connection with the human soul through poetry, intertwined with a few swear words, psychology, anthropology, and hopefully a good measure of humour. It is written in the first person, and I guess is somewhat of an autobiography of someone who has had a lot of life experience, and is a little bit "Aspie", as her friends might say.

Me: I am a swimmer, a nurse, a mother, a lover and a friend. I was also diagnosed with bipolar disorder at thirty-eight years of age, so have squeezed a lot into this manic life (some may liken it to babysitting an orangutang) and hopefully the author shall finish one's book (and hopefully one's computer will save it this time). The poems shall occupy each seemingly random yet perfectly ordered chapter of this book. I believe we all have something to teach each other.

Finally, this book is a journey underwritten by love. Yes, I guess I'm full hippy these days. But I really believe that you get the best and learn from people when you show them a bit of love. If you examine the spectrum of emotions they are founded in receiving love and not receiving love. A little bit of love goes a long way. Love is fundamental to the human soul, I feel the longer you live, the better you learn how to love, and the more you learn how to love unconditionally, if you want to. I believe that this is the journey of the soul.

Money

Once we hunters, gatherers, we roamed this land. We ran, and walked, and laughed, and played, and sang. We didn't have to navigate politics, ethics, capitalism, greed and money.

We were one, harmonious with the land, the ocean, the sky. We were invisible because we were part of a whole. Our hearts were full, we were enough.

Love was enough.

The earth was enough.

Mother nature was enough.

People were enough.

Take me back to when nothing was everything.

I believe money is evil. Just think how many evil things are done for money. The Credit Suisse Global Wealth Report (2021) states that the world's richest one percent, those with more than one million dollars, own 43.3 percent of the world's wealth. Their data also shows that adults with less than ten thousand dollars in wealth make up 53.6 percent of the world's population but hold just 1.4 percent of global wealth.

Coffee and Lust

You are my coffee.
You asked my where I'm at, Goddammit how can you not know?
My heart jumps out of my chest, I think I need some Adenosine.*
My lips are on fire,
my legs are wobbly,
my hands are trembling,
I try to deny it,
getting harder to breathe,
so you see,
I really don't need that coffee,
you are my coffee.

But really I am quite shy,
a little bit Aspie,
I pretend because I have learned how to over many, many lifetimes.
Touch means more to me, Rainman,
that's why I laughed,
I've already computed every possible outcome,
elation,
despair.
My mind runs like a show reel,
I dive deep,
I'm a daydreamer dreaming of you,
my mind drifts to total bliss,
pure ecstasy with every thrust,
wondering when I'll get my next sip,
because I can't breathe,
I can't sleep,
I can't eat,

until I get my next sip.

But I want much more than a sip,
I want to touch lips,
embrace,
I want to be your keep-me cup,
keep you warm and frothy as you do me.
Only matter,
without you I'd be a vacuum,
lost in spacetime,
but in naked singularity we can inflate the cosmos,
for in the darkness of night,
time is but an illusion,
only love is real.

Coffee?

*adenosine is a drug given for abnormal fast cardiac rhythms

I never really understood, or drank, coffee until I arrived in Melbourne. Then I succumbed to peer pressure, as it is really integrated into the Melburnian culture (yes, understatement I know). Now I'm somewhat of a coffee snob and can't really make it through the day without three long maccs. Coffee makes you feel alive. I'm not sure how I got to thirty without it. I bought a new coffee machine recently and had to stop myself from perfecting the art of coffee making after six coffees. Coffee wakes you up and makes you feel warm inside. I feel that the feeling you get from coffee is similar to lust. It gets your adrenaline going and your heart rate up. Coffee and lust, well that's an explosive combination. Don't try this at home kids!

Love

Tabla Gentleman

I swiped right,
he did the same.
He was waiting under the ACMI sign
but he was on the other side from mine,
waiting in parallel,
He took off his hat,
We circled Fed Square
from the river to the stairs,
the bars were all full
and so was my heart,
oh Gentleman
from the very start.

We found refuge at Beer Deluxe,
we talked and laughed and talked and talked
like old friends reunited,
giggling and overexcited.
We shared some food,
We shared the mood,
we wanted more,
so, we grabbed a late-night coffee,
things began to get a little frothy.

We made it to the train,
passed a crazy guy who yelled, "Fuck Off!"

Oh Melbourne,
there's nowhere the same.
I can't believe the time,
good job I'm not Cinderella.
Seriously though, who is this fella?

Then there were more
late night phone calls,
messages galore.
He put my hand on his gearknob,
oh heartthrob.
Tears of happiness,
colours so bright,
a giddy high,
a companionship that feels so right.

A beautiful thief,
he stole my sleep
but he gave so much more in return,
and now he's here
wherever I go,
deep inside
from head to toe.
Oh Gentleman, you should know that
You had me when you took off your hat.

Oh the sweet feeling of unconditional love! I don't really think I've experienced this love (except from my parents) until I turned forty and met a very sweet guy. My parents showed me unconditional love, with the occasional spanking that was for my own good. I would hope this is the reason I can reciprocate to others. My favourite song is *Oh Yoko!* by John Lennon. It's such a raw love song. It just portrays that love can be so simple. A deep respect. It's not about the big gestures, it's about those everyday little efforts you make for each other. That's what love is. Doing what you can for each other without judgement.

Ego

Formlessness

Let's go back,
back in (so-called) time,
back in space,
before we knew what we knew,
before we thought what we thought,
before society defined us.

There were no lines,
no curves,
no edges,
no hang ups,
just you
before you grew,
before you knew

too much.

Nirvana

Nowhere to be, nowhere to go,
nowhere to see, nothing to know,
feed the flower,
let it grow,
a thousand petals deep inside.
There's nowhere to run or hide,
man nor woman,
only one.
Go beyond,
seek and unlearn then relearn,
fall in love over and over again.
Think backwards,
don't be fooled by the constraints and construction of time.
Let the tree grow,
let life flow,
let form go,
let it be.
Let love lead,
soon you'll see,
everything will happen,
as it's meant to be,
judgement free,
East and West in harmony.

I don't have a particular denomination, but I do follow some of the Taoist and Buddhist philosophies.
Enlightenment is everything. So many connections. So many people.

Music

*Pause, take a moment,
listen to the music of the universe.
Inhale.
Bare feet connected through gravity,
but weightless with love.
Hear the waves crashing,
the birds singing,
the bees buzzing,
the trees rustling.*

*See the music of the universe,
colours dancing across the sky,
the trees swaying,
rainbow prisms,
reflections,
streams,
mountains.*

Feel the synchronicity of the universe.

Soul Woman

*She came dressed in white,
she goes between worlds,
an infinite mirror of consciousness.
She waves her wand,
she dives deep,
she'll try to tell you all the things she's seen,
but you're not listening,
not hard enough.*

*Move in closer,
look into her eyes,
delve into her psyche.
Stop time itself.
She is the past,
the present, the future,
but she's already gone.
She moves beyond time
and her time is fast
because she knows too much,
she's seen too much.*

*She's a goddess,
she's a sorceress,
she's a healer,
she runs with wolves,
she's a wild woman.
Let her be.*

See the work she can do,
let her wear her cloak of invisibility,
but when she's ready
see her,
all of her,
give her some love,
and set her free.

Let her go home,
let her roam,
let her laugh,
let her cry,
let her emotions flow,
for
only
then you will know
her.

She who bears,
she who cares,
she who gives and gives,
and loves and loves.
Warrior.
Let her go home,
even for a short time,
let her rest that thoughtful mind.

Coronavirus and Mother Earth

And in delving into her psyche she removed toilet roll
after toilet roll,
everything she had been hoarding up until this moment,
and she descended into nothingness.
Nowhere to go,
nothing to see,
no-one to meet,
just her.
She could
just
be
and with this
she was truly,
finally,
completely
free.

Lady Anxiety

She comes in waves,
I am her slave,
I let her in,
so we begin,
the dance.
Inch by inch,
Feel her pinch,
I sit with her,
we talk inside,
nowhere to run or hide,
but slowly I starve her of my time,
soon time will once again become mine.
The less I think,
the more she shrinks,
I'm no longer on the brink,
of self-destruction.
I put her out,
I feel her pout,
she is no longer me,
once more I can see,
the rose is free,
return to synchronicity.

An Ode to the Swimming Pool

Oh swimming pool,
how I have missed thee so.
The ocean felt good
but how I longed for thine sharp lines and formidable edges,
how my toes caress the grout between your tiles between sets,
that long straight black line to infinity,
that twenty-eight whole degrees of Celsius,
the taste of chlorine on my tongue,
the bubbles which tickle my cheek with each catch,
the concentric circles from each falling droplet from my fingers before
they break the surface.
The woosh and hum of liquid immersion,
miles upon miles travelled in a single container,
numbers and time,
turn after turn,
ripples of light across the floor.
Can I say more?
Swimming pool,

my home.

Lockdown Three

Apocalypse is inevitable now.
I have six toilet rolls, and have resorted to tinned food, until my meal
delivery arrives tomorrow.
My overlord should make contact shortly and beam me up to the tenth
dimension.
The kids think it's the best day of their life, they have been on their
iPads for half the day in their knickers.
I've lost all sense of time,
and space.

High

Oh little caterpillar, where are you going?
Down and round, and up the spout,
can you tell me what this world is about?

Together we can reach the stars,
don't stop to smell the roses,
we don't need to read sheet music,
together we can be free,
we can write our very own symphony.

Shhhh, don't listen.
Breathe,
don't worry,
nothing's gonna change,
we have time,
soon we go.

Listen to the music,
intonation after intonation,
pure love.
Take your time with me.
In every story ever told,
ten dimensions
in the human factory.
Lose yourself in the music,
leave the roses behind,
but keep on dancing and singing and acting.
Most of all stay kind.

Relax, and go with the flow,
ride the wave,
for all you can do,
is just be you,
one with the earth, sea and sky,
you can never aim too high.
Don't be a robot,
lose yourself in the language of the ancient storytellers,
then find yourself again,
home sweet home.
It was here the whole time,
you just weren't looking hard enough.

Welcome home, Goldilocks, you are so loved.
We've been waiting for you.

You, beautiful you.

We Got Time (Awake)

We didn't want it,
but we got it.
What to do with it?
You always said, "I haven't got time."

Now don't be sad,
there's fun to be had.
Let's get to know each other again,
let's be bored with each other,
let's write some poems,
let's make some art,
it doesn't have to be perfect,
it just has to be authentic,
like you.

Let's strip it back,
remove the veils,
show me your real face,
I'll take you to my happy place,
let's hold each other's space,
let's go back in time,
see what we can find.

Timelessness

Oh relentless time,
you run and run
and I can't seem to catch you.
You are too swift for me,
too agile,
too bold.
If only you could just halt for one sweet moment,
then we could not be defined by you,
your clocks,
your watches,
your numbers,
ever turning,
ever ticking,
ever clicking,
ever dominating.
I'm falling behind,
oh please be kind,
untouchable,
but always in mind.
I fear I will never fathom you,
sweet,
imposing,
vanquishing,
time.

Vacuum

Oh to be a vacuum,
but which kind of vacuum?
I'm not sure which one,
the kinds that sucks up dirt and dust
or the kind that leads one to oblivion.
Do I feed on the unwanted remnants everyone has left behind,
or up above?
Am I devoid of anything?
No love,
no time,
for at least the remnants have seen love
felt the weight of gravity.
I do wonder if I'd be annoyed
existing as a cosmic void,
or will I be at peace
with all pressure released?
Would ignorance be bliss,
never knowing a single kiss?

A Night with Oneself

I don't have to cook,
I don't have to talk (with my mouth),
I don't have to endure,
I don't have to ignore,
I don't have to implore,
I don't have to entertain,
I don't have to nurse,
I don't have to mirror,
I don't have to act,
I don't have to cheer,
I don't have to. I don't have to.

It's just me and the infinite multiverse,
a thousand fairy-tales,
billions of neurons firing,
memories flickering,
question after question,
feelings recurring,
chest rising and falling,
heart sounds dual,
pulsating fingertips and toes,
breeze through my hairs,
hairs like a forest,
rooted above the most complex beautiful cosmos.

An Empath's Poem: Music of the Heart

Lub dub,
left and right,
listen the music of the night.

Head on your chest,
together we rest,
getting good flows,
from head to toe.

Dancing and swaying,
nothing needs saying,
always playing

PQRS,
up and down.
Beep. Beep. Beeeep. Beep.

Can you feel his heartbeat?

Pigeon

Oh, pigeon in yonder window,
all alone
on your telegraph wire,
I hope it wasn't your mate
that met her fate
by a house cat
who got a little bit fat
because of her owner
who overindulges her,
so was it the cat or the owner
that indeed
led the pigeon to her fate?

Oh pigeon, I hope you're not lonely on my account,
if only I hadn't put those cat biscuits out.
Oh, how one thought becomes an action,
a cascade,
a ripple of reaction,
a crime in time,
a step-in space.
Oh pigeon,
I'm truly sorry this was the case,
my intentions were good
but fate, as it were,
not.

Black, Red and Yellow

Murder,
millions of pure animal spirits,
sorry is not enough.
Give back the water,
give back the land,
evacuate,
genocide
omnicide.
The apocalypse is now.
Sixty thousand years to build humanity,
two hundred years to decimate it.
A constitution of man-made drought,
an entire country sold out.
Avatar: in real life.

You can take her heart,
you can take her spirit,
but she will breathe again,
She will breathe life again,
she will breathe love again,
she will dream again.

Newton knew it,
she knows it,
she grows it,
she will make order from the chaos,
she will return this land to its rightful owners,
to those that know they cannot "own" this land, this ocean, this sky,
this Mother Earth.

Nothing

*Let's do nothing,
we've got time.*

Corona: the Funeral

I sit in thought
back in Freedom,
yearning for my former life
on the vacation that nobody wanted.
I peek inside cars just to see people's naked faces,
Oh, what a thrill,
it gives me a chill
whilst we wait out this coronavirus.

Invisible Nurse

*I see you
but you don't see me,
that's okay,
that's how it's supposed to be.*

I waited until you left.

Patterns 28/1/22

And once again I see,
we are about to repeat history.
A tired world
has unfurled,
politicians at odds,
giving war the nod.
Where are you now?
Oh Gods,
heaven has become hell,
somebody ring the bell.
Please not again,
I can't do it again,
all that pain,
all that loss,
yet we still watch
the world
unfurl.
Seven billion of us
only to wage war,
we've learned nothing from before,
please, please we must implore,
stop
the
Third
World
War.

Walk the Human

It's time to walk the human,
let's go to the human park.
If he's good
I might let him off the lead,
but only
if he pleads.
Let's walk the human,
I hope he doesn't poop,
I'll have to pick it up,
and put it in a plastic bag
and
I was going to grow potatoes
but now it goes to landfill in a plastic bag.
It's time to walk the human.
This world is fucked.

Intensive Care Nursing

*This nursing
it has changed me.
I often wonder
what life my life would have been like
if I had not seen the things that I have seen.
so many times,
so many lives,
so many husbands,
so many wives,
so many children,
so many babies,
so many judged
as being "crazy"
when really they were in pain,
they couldn't do it all over again.
Riding the rollercoaster,
teetering on the brink of life and death,
watching their loved take their last breath.*

*We are all big children
wondering when and why life got so hard,
having to make the big decisions,
fraught
with pain,*

lessons we are not taught.

Lost Socks of the Psyche

*There it is,
another one
stuck out there,
in there.
Where is your pair?
Hey, you there?
Who said I need a pair?
Au contraire
my friend,
I will not bend
to conform
even to keep you
a little warmer
inside.
I will not hide
or diminish
my pride
just so
I can look neat
on your feet.
My friends are all odd
and I like it like that,
they've all got a bit more fluff
and that's the way its gonna stay
because,
you know what?
Life's better that way.*

Cockatoo

Look at you
cockatoo,
be careful
or they'll put you in the zoo
and make you talk,
you see,
humans don't understand the squark.
They take your friends,
there is no end
to their entrapment,
destruction,
despair.
They can never be satisfied
with what they have inside
or outside.
Only when
the Sixth Mass Extinction reveals, divulges our ever-shifting baselines
into nothingness
will we see
that we had time
to collectively change
history.

The Beat

Oh, cargo ship
Where have you been?
O'er oceans vast and wild seas?
I'd love to see the storms you've fought
just in order
to have brought
the people their stuff,
tossing and turning
like a toy boat,
huge,
yet remains afloat.
I wonder what it is you have onboard
that one should risk their very life for.
Is it for adventure?
Is it for money?
Surely it's not for some kid's plastic Barbie.
I can't imagine all the things you'd see
just to bring the goods of humanity,
even pirates,
oh what a treat
to be
off the
monotonous
downtrodden
path
of
the
routine
beat.

Lilly (Cat)

Cat: Meow meow meow.
Me: It's twelve o'clock, you know you don't get fed until 4 o'clock.
Cat: Meow.
Me: I told you, four o'clock.
Cat: Meow meow meowww.
Me: Here have some cat biscuits.
Cat: Meow meow.
Me: I told you four o'clock.
Three-thirty p.m. Cat: Meow meow meow.
Me: Here just have your food.
Cat: Meow.

Ethics of a Poet

I'm a poet
don't you know,
I decide
how high
or
how low
it goes,
up
and
down,
left or right.
Come along guys,
hold on tight.
Are you with me?
I feel your pain
deep inside
my brain,
one can only feign
that one does not give a shit.

An Illusion

What if this life were an illusion?
Nothing but confusion
but really a test
to see if we can move onto the next
where Mother Earth is Queen,
for as far as can be seen,
she rules all
and we've all been screened
to be gentle
and take care of everything.
We hum and sing
like birds and bees,
no need for locks and keys,
Here we speak love
and all is shared,
all is cared
for
by
us.

The Lovers.